ULTIMATE
PUZZLE CHALLENGE

Head Twisters

By
Helene Hovanec

Illustrated by
Gary LaCoste

STERLING

New York / London
www.sterlingpublishing.com/kids

STERLING and the distinctive Sterling logo are registered trademarks of Sterling Publishing Co., Inc.

Lot #: 10 9 8 7 6 5 4 3 2 1
09/10

Published by Sterling Publishing Co., Inc.
387 Park Avenue South, New York, NY 10016
© 2010 by Helene Hovanec
Illustrations by Gary LaCoste
Distributed in Canada by Sterling Publishing
$C/_o$ Canadian Manda Group, 165 Dufferin Street
Toronto, Ontario, Canada M6K 3H6
Distributed in the United Kingdom by GMC Distribution Services
Castle Place, 166 High Street, Lewes, East Sussex, England BN7 1XU
Distributed in Australia by Capricorn Link (Australia) Pty. Ltd.
P.O. Box 704, Windsor, NSW 2756, Australia

Sterling ISBN 978-1-4027-6206-2

For information about custom editions, special sales, premium and corporate purchases, please contact Sterling Special Sales Department at 800-805-5489 or specialsales@sterlingpublishing.com.

Designed by Kate Moll

INTRODUCTION

Welcome to the **Ultimate Puzzle Challenge**—a series of books for children who love word searches, crisscrosses, mazes, crosswords, and variety puzzles. As an added bonus, many puzzles are based on silly riddles that will make you giggle or smile.

I hope **Head Twisters** will amuse and challenge you at the same time. You may whiz through some puzzles in just a few minutes, but others might make your brain work overtime. There are no rules to follow except the directions before each puzzle, so go through the book at your own pace. If you don't know something, it's okay to ask for help, use a dictionary, or even peek at the answer—these are all good ways to learn! The main goal is to have fun and exercise your brain.

Take the **Ultimate Puzzle Challenge** . . . and enjoy!

—Helene Hovanec

LETTER BOXES

Riddle: **What do you get when you cross a centipede with a parrot?**

To find the answer to this riddle, put the missing letters in the grid to create words that make sense both across and down. Then copy those letters onto the same-numbered blanks below and read from 1 to 13.

Answer:

$\overline{}\ \ \overline{}\ \overline{}\ \overline{}\ \overline{}\ \overline{}\ \overline{}\ \ \overline{}\ \overline{}\ \overline{}\ \overline{}\ \overline{}\ \overline{}$
 1   2 3 4 5 6 7   8 9 10 11 12 13

Answer on page 87.

HOUSE HUNTING

How fast can you get through this house maze?

ENTER

EXIT

Answer on page 96.

ICE IS NICE

The word ICE is used in each word in the right column. Read each clue and fill in the letters to complete the answer word.

1. Round shape   __ I __ C __ E

2. Small cubes used in games   __ I C E

3. Fruity drink   __ __ I C E

4. A room for cooking   __ I __ C __ E __

5. Small rodents   __ I C E

6. Five-cent coin   __ I C __ E __

7. Place of business   __ __ __ I C E

8. _____ of cake (easy to do)   __ I __ C E

9. People who enforce the law   __ __ __ I C E

10. What something costs   __ __ I C E

11. Son of a king   __ __ I __ C E

12. Wealthier   __ I C __ E __

13. Halloween figures with pointed black hats   __ I __ C __ E __

14. Devices for turning lights on and off   __ __ I __ C __ E __

Answers on page 87.

ADD-A-LETTER

Add one letter to each line and rearrange some of the letters to make words that answer the clues.

———
The twentieth letter of the alphabet

——— ———
What the symbol @ stands for

——— ——— ———
Had food

——— ——— ——— ———
Opposite of love

——— ——— ——— ——— ———
Valentine symbol

——— ——— ——— ——— ——— ———
Warming device

——— ——— ——— ——— ——— ——— ———
Dishonest person

——— ——— ——— ——— ——— ——— ——— ———
Instructors

Answers on page 91.

CLOTHES ENCOUNTERS

Nineteen articles of clothing are hidden in the box below. Look up, down, and diagonally, both forward and backward, to discover them all. Circle each word when you find it.

BLOUSE
CAPE
DRESS
HAT
JEANS
JUMPER
KILT
RAINCOAT
ROBE
SHIRT
SKIRT
SLICKER
SOCKS
SUIT
SWEATER
TIE
TROUSERS
TURTLENECK
TUXEDO

R	J	S	S	W	E	A	T	E	R
O	E	Z	R	S	K	I	R	T	A
D	N	K	L	E	E	L	Z	A	I
E	S	O	C	K	S	R	T	H	N
X	S	B	V	I	E	U	D	G	C
U	N	L	Y	P	L	V	O	A	O
T	A	O	M	R	K	S	P	R	A
L	E	U	R	O	B	E	U	Z	T
I	J	S	H	I	R	T	Z	I	X
K	C	E	N	E	L	T	R	U	T

OUT OF SIGHT

Eight things that kids might use when they visit the zoo are hidden in the scene on the opposite page. Can you find all of them?

Answers on page 96.

STARTERS

Figure out the answer to each clue and write only the first letter in its numbered box in the grid on the facing page. When the puzzle is complete, read from 1 to 12 to find a four-word phrase that means "in fine shape."

_____ Angeles, California   (Box 11)

Second month   (Box 1)

Art stand used to hold paintings   (Box 12)

Language spoken in Rome   (Box 2)

Eighth month   (Box 6)

Not costing anything   (Box 7)

Liquid in fountain pens   (Box 8)

Reptile similar to a crocodile   (Box 4)

Rumbling sound that follows lightning   (Box 3)

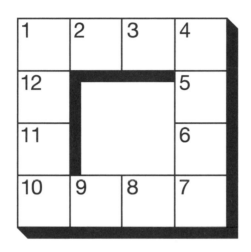

Doctor who takes care of your teeth   (Box 10)

The day after Friday   (Box 5)

Food, like cake or pie, served at
the end of a meal   (Box 9)

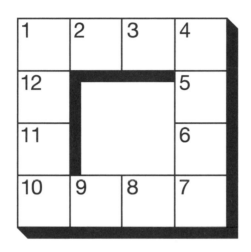

1	2	3	4
12			5
11			6
10	9	8	7

Answers on page 87.

SAFETY FIRST

Use this code to find a riddle and its answer.

A = ∨		N = ⟨⟨	
B = ◀		O = ⊙	
C = ←		P = ✿	
D = ❏		Q = ♥	
E = ▽		R = ↙	
F = ☎		S = ✪	
G = ✷		T = ■	
H = ▲		U = ⊕	
I = ◉		V = Ø	
J = ✈		W = ✂	
K = ☞		X = ♠	
L = ❖		Y = ↑	
M = }		Z = △	

�〄 ▲ ∨ ■    ❑ ⬅

✳ ▲ ⬅ ✪ ■ ✪    ❑ ⬅

✄ ▲ ▽ ⬔    ■ ▲ ▽ ↑    ✳ ▽ ■

◉ ⬔ ■ ⬅    ∨   ⬅ ∨ ⬐ ?

■ ▲ ▽ ↑   ☎ ∨ ✪ ■ ▽ ⬔

■ ▲ ▽ ◉ ⬐   ✪ ▲ ▽ ▽ ■

◀ ▽ ❖ ■ ✪.

Answers on page 93.

FOUL BALL

Read each clue and cross off its definition on the opposite page. Then write the leftover words, from left to right and top to bottom, on the line. They won't make any sense at first. But . . . change one letter in each word to find the answer to this riddle: **Why wasn't Cinderella allowed to play on the baseball team?**

CLUES

1. Newspaper worker
2. Large serving dish
3. A woman's handbag
4. Type of puzzle
5. Hard
6. Wide city street
7. Dinner
8. Type of snake
9. Perhaps
10. Small flute
11. Painting of a person
12. Take it easy
13. Keep apart
14. Not deep
15. Small house made of logs
16. Sad
17. Awful
18. Brave
19. Silent

DIFFICULT	PICCOLO	BOULEVARD	PLATTER	SHY
TERRIBLE	POCKETBOOK	MAN	COURAGEOUS	COBRA
SEPARATE	SWAY	CABIN	SUPPER	FROG
UNHAPPY	PORTRAIT	SHE	RELAX	MAYBE
JIGSAW	SHALLOW	REPORTER	WALL	QUIET

Leftover words:

_____

Change one letter in each word:

_____

Answer on page 86.

SOUND OFF

Fill in the grid with words that **SOUND** like the listed words but that have different meanings and that are spelled differently. Then read **DOWN** the starred column to find things that make very loud sounds. The first one was done for you.

1. LONE
2. FORTH
3. BILLED
4. SALE
5. LEASED
6. SUM
7. FARE
8. WEAK
9. SERIAL
10. REEL
11. PAWS

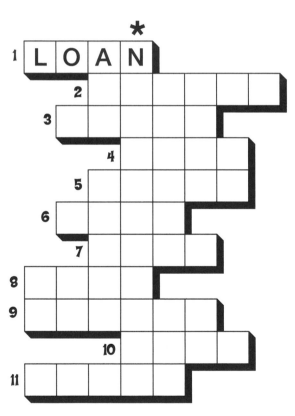

Answers on page 88.

FRONT OF THE LINE

Answer each clue with a five-letter word and write it in the blanks. Then read down the first column to find a term describing an important, influential person.

Clue	Blanks
Small mountains	_ _ _ _ _
One dozen minus four	_ _ _ _ _
Opposite of subtracted	_ _ _ _ _
When you're asleep, you might have a . . .	_ _ _ _ _
Conceals	_ _ _ _ _
Unlocks a door	_ _ _ _ _
Between eighth and tenth	_ _ _ _ _
Object used for writing on blackboards	_ _ _ _ _
Back parts of feet	_ _ _ _ _
Large body of water, like the Arctic	_ _ _ _ _

Answer: _____

Answers on page 90.

WAKE-UP CALL

Write one letter in the blank space on each line to form a nine-letter word. Then read down the column to find the answer to this riddle: **What does a chicken farmer use to wake up in the morning?**

```
N E C T _ R I N E
A T T E _ T I O N

C O M P _ N I O N
K N O W _ E D G E
S I G N _ T U R E
G E O G _ A P H Y
C H I P _ U N K S

B I C Y _ L I S T
M I S P _ A C E D
G R A D _ A L L Y
D E M O _ R A C Y
C H E E _ B O N E
```

Answer on page 90.

TENNIS ANYONE?

Circle the two pictures that are alike.

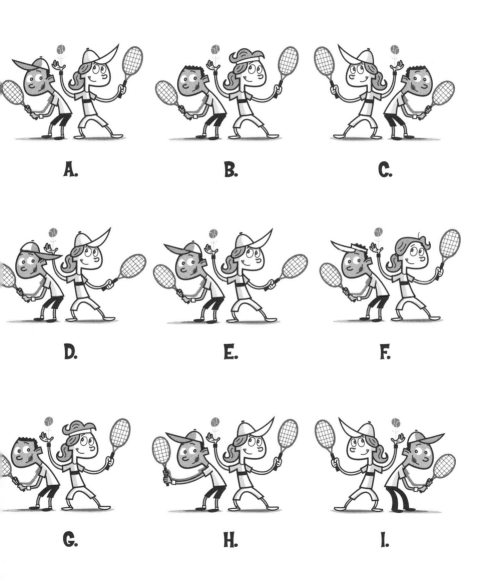

A.

B.

C.

D.

E.

F.

G.

H.

I.

Answer on page 94.

ON THE OUTSKIRTS

Place one of the four-letter words from the box below around the correct letter groups in the left-hand column to make a seven-letter word that fits the clue in the right-hand column. Keep the letters you write in the same order.

Example: C O S T U M E   something worn on Halloween

BALL	COST	DEED	FILE
	LOST	REST	
RUSH	SEAL	THEN	WEST

1. __ __ U D E __ __   noisiest

2. __ __ V E R __ __   quite a few

3. __ __ A K E __ __   having the least strength

4. __ __ R B E __ __   weightlifter's equipment

5. __ __ X A B __ __   can be repaired

6. __ __ N T E __ __   a competition

7. __ __ C I D __ __   made up one's mind

8. __ __ B B I __ __   trash

9. __ __ Q U E __ __   ask for

10. __ __ I C K __ __   to make something less thin

Answers on page 96.

STEP BY STEP

To find a riddle and its answer, start at the circled letter in the grid and move one square at a time. Move straight across, up, or down, but not diagonally. Write each letter in the blank space when you find it, and cross it off in the grid. The letters and symbols in the grid are used only once.

H __ __   __ __ __ __

__   __ __ __ __ __ __

__ __ __ __   __

__ __ __ __ __ __ ?

__ __   __

__ __ __ __ __ __ __ __ __ __ .

I	N	.	E
?	A	O	P
R	H	L	E
E	E	N	V
T	L	A	L
T	E	A	I
O	(H)	M	N
W	D	O	E
A	S	E	K
C	H	I	C

Answers on page 89.

PICTURE CROSSWORD

Name each picture and write it in the numbered spaces going **ACROSS** or **DOWN**.

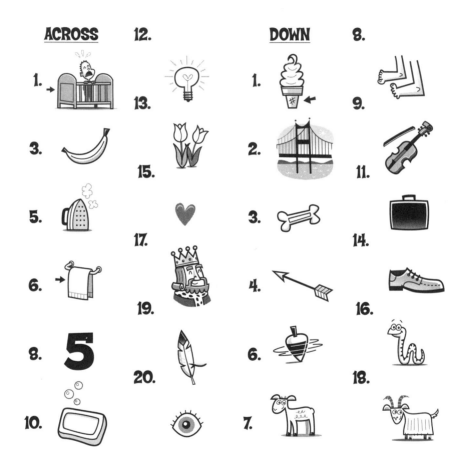

TWOSOMES

Each word in the box will answer the two different clues on one line. Find the word in the box and write it in the grid on the opposite page, making sure you place it in the correct line. (Note: sometimes the words will be pronounced differently.) Then read down one of the columns to find things that always come in pairs.

CRANE	DOVE	FAST	HIVES
KING	PUNCH	REMOTE	SAFE
SPRINKLES		TICK	

---

1. Hit hard / fruit drink

2. Bees' homes / itchy skin problem

3. Bird of peace / plunged into the water

4. Light rains / ice cream toppings

5. Free from danger / container for valuables

6. Far away / TV device

7. Insect / clock sound

8. Wading bird / machine used at construction sites

9. Royal man / Chess piece

10. Go without eating / speedy

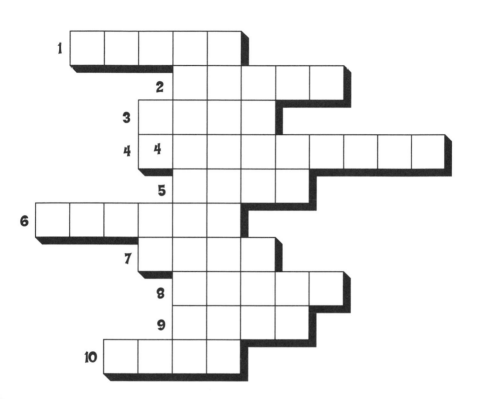

Answers on page 88.

CLOSE CALLS

To complete the words in the right column, fill in the blanks with a word that means the same thing as the word in the left column. Then move the numbered letters to the same-numbered blanks below to find some people who are close to you.

GRAB   M I S __ __ __ __ N
                            4   8

HURRY   H A I R B __ __ __ __
                              6   3

FINISH   C A L __ __ __ A R
                              9 10

DISTANT   __ __ __ E W E L L
                          5

TEAR   T __ __ __ L E T S
                           7

CERTAIN   T R E A __ __ __ __
                             11   2

SMASH   __ __ __ __ __ F A S T
                       1

Answer: __ __ __ __   __ __ __ __ __ __ __
           1   2   3   4   5   6   7   8   9 10 11

Answers on page 88.

DOUBLE TROUBLE

Separate the word list into two categories: words that rhyme with "go" and words that rhyme with "stay." Then fit the words into the grid in which they belong. Each grid will only contain words from one category. A few letters were already placed to get you started.

AWAY
BELOW
BOUQUET
DOE
DOUGH
GRAY
GROW
OBEY
PAY
PREY
SEW
SLEIGH
THEY
THOUGH
THROW
WEIGH
WHOA

L

W

Answers on page 88.

QUICK CHANGES

Change just one letter in each word to make a new word that fits the clue. Write the new word in the third column and the new letter in the fourth. Then take the new letters only and write them in the same-numbered blanks to answer this riddle: **Where do students in New York City learn their multiplication tables?** The first one has been done for you.

$5 \times 5 = 25$

$3 \times 4 =$

$7 \times 2 =$

$6 \times 3 = 18$

WORD	CLUE	NEW WORD	NEW LETTER
FLAME	Picture holder	FRAME	R 12
PEDAL	Prize given at the Olympics	_____	____ 5
SWEAT	Sugary	_____	____ 13
MARKS	Face disguises	_____	____ 7
FALLS	Gets an "F"	_____	____ 1
HIRED	Sleepy	_____	____ 3
MONTH	Face part	_____	____ 10
BRAND	Hair style	_____	____ 4
SMALL	Use your nose	_____	____ 6
RAVES	Rescues	_____	____ 8
RIGHT	Evening	_____	____ 2
GUEST	Search	_____	____ 9
CURVE	Cut up a turkey	_____	____ 11

Answer: $\overline{}_1 \overline{}_2 \quad \overline{}_3 \overline{}_4 \overline{}_5 \overline{}_6 \overline{}_7 \quad \overline{}_8 \overline{}_9 \overline{}_{10} \overline{}_{11} \overline{R}_{12} \overline{}_{13}$

Answers on page 90.

DIRECTIONAL SIGNALS

Put your finger on the circled letter and follow the directions given below to move your finger all around the grid. Use the directional arrows on the left to guide your finger. When you land on a letter, write it down in the blank next to that clue and continue from that letter. Then read down to answer this riddle: **What did the jack say to the car?**

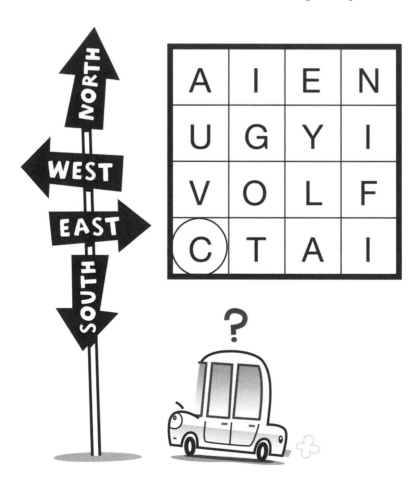

Start with the circled letter   <u> c </u>

Move two spaces east   _____

Move one space east and three spaces north   _____

Move one space south   _____

Move two spaces west   _____

Move one space north   _____

Move one space west and two spaces south   _____

Move two spaces east and two spaces north   _____

Move one space south   _____

Move one space south and one space west   _____

Move one space west and one space north   _____

Move one space north   _____

Move two spaces east and two spaces south   _____

Move one space east and one space south   _____

Move one space north   _____

Move two spaces west and one space south   _____

Answer: _____

Answer on page 86.

IT'S NOT WHAT YOU SAY . . .

...it's how you say it. Each of the following ten boxes contains words or letters that create coded messages. Look at the size of the letters and words, the direction they're facing, and other visual clues to unlock their secrets.

Example: BEND   = bend over backward
        DRAW

1.

> # DEAL

_____

2.

| T | H | H | A | N | G | E | R | E |

_____

3.

> ## BAN   ANA

_____

4.

> story

_____

5.

THE RUG
SWEEP IT

_____

6.

R E T R A U Q

_____

7.

PARK PARK

_____

8.

HANDED

_____

9.

THE JACK BOX

_____

10. YOU JUST ME

_____

Answers on page 87.

READING ROOM

Answer each clue and write the word on the blanks. Then move each letter to its same-numbered blank on the opposite page. Work back and forth between the clues and the answer to find a riddle and its answer.

CLUES

1. Opposite of north

— — — — —
29 22 10 25 2

2. Mittens are worn on these

— — — — —
45 32 43 14 19

3. A 365-day period

— — — —
39 28 30 38

4. 12 inches = one ____

— — — —
11 16 7 24

5. What we breathe

— — —
37 34 4

6. Animal like "grizzly" or "black"

— — — —
35 3 42 41

7. The color of a log

— — — — —
21 26 17 1 13

8. Sob

— — —
44 36 8

9. What a mean dog might do

‾‾ ‾‾ ‾‾ ‾‾
40 12 31 5

10. Cook in an oven

‾‾ ‾‾ ‾‾ ‾‾
15 20 18 27

11. Noisy

‾‾ ‾‾ ‾‾ ‾‾
33 9 23 6

‾‾ ‾‾ ‾‾ ‾‾ ‾‾   ‾‾ ‾‾   ‾‾ ‾‾ ‾‾
1 2 3 4 5   .6 7   8 9 10

‾‾ ‾‾ ‾‾ ‾‾   ‾‾ ‾‾ ‾‾ ‾‾ ‾‾   ‾‾ ‾‾ ‾‾ ‾‾ ‾‾
11 12 13 14   15 16 17 18 19   20 21 22 23 24

‾‾ ‾‾ ‾‾ ‾‾ ‾‾ ?
25 26 27 28 29

‾‾ ‾‾   ‾‾   ‾‾ ‾‾ ‾‾ ‾‾ ‾‾ ‾‾   ‾‾
30 31   32   33 34 35 36 37 38   39

‾‾ ‾‾ ‾‾ ‾‾ ‾‾ ‾‾ .
40 41 42 43 44 45

Answers on page 88.

FILM CLIP

Number the pictures from 1 to 8 to make a story without words.

Answers on page 93.

CLOCKWORK

The word in the right column uses all the letters of the word in the left column EXCEPT for one letter. Write the missing letter on the blank. Then write the letters on the blanks below to find the four-word answer to this riddle:

Why wasn't the clock allowed in the library?

CLEAREST	___	(5)	RELATES
ARTICLES	___	(1)	SCARLET
CRACKERS	___	(6)	SCARCER
CREATURE	___	(13)	TERRACE
EPISODES	___	(4)	DESPISE
SHUTTLES	___	(9)	SLEUTHS
MATTRESS	___	(3)	STREAMS
OPERATED	___	(11)	TAPERED
PLATTERS	___	(2)	PLASTER
READINGS	___	(8)	ERASING
REGIMENT	___	(12)	INTEGER
CRUMBLES	___	(14)	SLUMBER
RELEASED	___	(7)	LEADERS
SMOOTHER	___	(10)	THERMOS
THICKEST	___	(15)	TICKETS

Answer: __ __ __ __ __ __ __ __
     1 2   3 4 5 6 7 8

__ __ __ __ __ __ __.
9 10 11 12 13 14 15

Answers on page 90.

SECRET CITIES

The name of one American city is hidden between two or three words in each silly sentence. Underline each one when you find it. Use the hints in the box to help you locate the cities.

1. SANTA CLAUS TINKERED IN HIS WORKSHOP.
2. WILL THEY SHIP THE GAZEBOS TONIGHT?
3. IS THE GARDEN VERY BEAUTIFUL?
4. SHE'S FROM A HARBOR TOWN.
5. BUY A STAMP AT THE POST OFFICE.
6. THEY MADE A CHART FOR DAD.
7. JUNE AUCTIONED OFF HER BOOKS.
8. CAN THE AUTHOR LAND ONE PLANE?
9. GIVE THE ADMIRAL EIGHT DOLLARS.
10. THE SCANDAL LASTED A LONG TIME.

HINTS

Capital of Colorado
City on the west coast of Florida
Capital of Connecticut
Largest city in Nebraska
Capital of Texas
Home of the Red Sox
Capital of Alaska
Texas city whose nickname is "Big D"
Capital of North Carolina
Florida city with many tourist attractions

Answers on page 93.

PICTURE RIDDLE

Write the word for each picture on the blanks below it.
Then copy the numbered letters to the same-numbered
blanks below for the answer to this riddle: **What is the best
thing to have after a very big meal?**

A.

$\overline{\ }\ \overline{\ }\ \overline{\ }\ \overline{\ }$
2 17 11

B.

$\overline{\ }\ \overline{\ }\ \overline{\ }\ \overline{\ }\ \overline{\ }\ \overline{\ }$
12 1   8 3 4

C.

$\overline{\ }\ \overline{\ }\ \overline{\ }\ \overline{\ }$
9   15

D.

$\overline{\ }\ \overline{\ }\ \overline{\ }\ \overline{\ }\ \overline{\ }$
13 7   16

E.

$\overline{\ }\ \overline{\ }\ \overline{\ }\ \overline{\ }$
6 14   5

F.

$\overline{\ }\ \overline{\ }\ \overline{\ }\ \overline{\ }\ \overline{\ }\ \overline{\ }$
10 18

Answer: $\overline{\ }$ $\overline{\ }\ \overline{\ }\ \overline{\ }\ \overline{\ }$ $\overline{\ }\ \overline{\ }\ \overline{\ }$
1   2 3 4 5   6 7 8

$\overline{\ }\ \overline{\ }\ \overline{\ }\ \overline{\ }\ \overline{\ }\ \overline{\ }\ \overline{\ }\ \overline{\ }\ \overline{\ }\ \overline{\ }$
9 10 11 12 13 14 15 16 17 18

Answers on page 95.

FIVERS

Your mission is to find five related five-letter words hidden in each small grid below—musical instruments in grid A and body parts in grid B. To find all the words, choose one letter from each column, moving from left to right. Each letter will be used once, so circle each one as you use it. Write the words next to the grid.

MUSICAL INSTRUMENTS

1. __BUGLE__
2. _____
3. _____
4. _____
5. _____

A.

B	A	A	J	E
F	U	U	L	E
C	I	N	N	O
P	L	L	L	O
B	E	G	T	O

BODY PARTS

1. _____
2. _____
3. _____
4. _____
5. _____

B.

B	N	U	R	N
A	R	A	T	W
H	O	B	I	H
M	E	K	L	T
E	L	A	O	E

Answers on page 94.

FAMILY ROOM FUN

Take a break in this family room to find and circle the names of the ten objects below.

Bookcase	Carpet	Couch
Curtain	Fireplace	Lamp
	Mirror	Plant
	Table	Television

Answers on page 92.

GO FIGURE

Figure out the number that answers each clue. You'll see that each number is equal to a letter, creating a code. Fill in each numbered blank below with the letter in the code that it stands for (numbers may be used more than once) to get the answer to this riddle: **What paper do reptiles read?**

Number of hours in a day ___ = H

Number of original U.S. colonies ___ = L

Number of levels on a double-decker bus ___ = T

Number of minutes in ¼ hour ___ = S

Number of days in June ___ = N

Number of nickels in a dollar ___ = C

Number of days in a week ___ = W

Number of people in a quartet ___ = A

Number of years in a decade ___ = E

Number of sides in a triangle ___ = Y

Answer:

$\overline{2}$ $\overline{24}$ $\overline{10}$ $\overline{15}$ $\overline{20}$ $\overline{4}$ $\overline{13}$ $\overline{3}$ $\overline{30}$ $\overline{10}$ $\overline{7}$ $\overline{15}$

Answers on page 89.

SOME DIFFERENCE

Circle eleven differences between the picture on this page and the one on the opposite page.

RIGHT ON "Q"

How quickly can you place each "Q" word in the grid? Start with the given letters and work from there until the grid is complete.

4 Letters
AQUA
QUIT

5 Letters
EQUAL
EQUIP
QUACK
QUAIL
SQUAD

6 Letters
LIQUID
OPAQUE
QUARTZ
QUILTS
QUIVER
SEQUEL

7 Letters
ANTIQUE
EQUATOR
REQUEST
SQUEAKY

8 Letters
QUARRELS
QUARTERS
QUICKEST
REQUIRES

SQUEAK

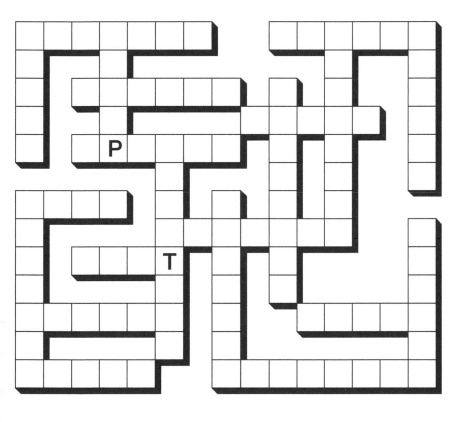

MEETING POINTS

Riddle: **Why are elephants so wrinkled?**

Write the word for each picture in the horizontal row of the grid that has the matching number. Then, to answer the riddle, look at the letter-number combination below each line in the riddle answer. Find the letters in the grid with the same combinations and write them in the blank spaces. (Not all the letters in the grid are used in the answers.)

Example: The first letter of the answer is labeled 4A. The letter to put above that line is the letter in the grid where the number 4 and the letter A meet.

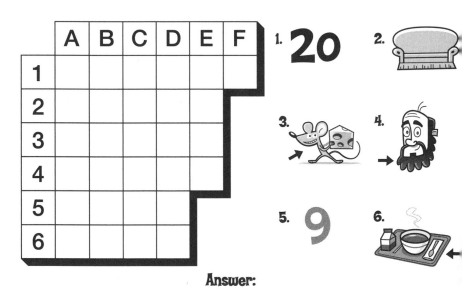

	A	B	C	D	E	F
1						
2						
3						
4						
5						
6						

1. **20**
2.
3.
4.
5. **9**
6.

Answer:

__ __ __ __ __ __ __   __ __ __   __ __ __ , __
4A 3E 2A 6C 2C 3D 5D   1F 2B 3C   2D 4C 1D   1A

            __ __ __ __   __ __ __ __ .
            5B 6B 3B 5C   6A 2E 1C 3A

Answers on page 86.

TIME OFF

Looking for places to go or things to do in your spare time? Put a letter on each blank to complete the words and name some of these things. Then read down the column to find a fun, but challenging, party activity.

FE __ TIVAL

CON __ ERT

PAR __ DE

CARNI __ AL

L __ CTURE

COU __ TY FAIR

MA __ IC SHOW

ROD __ O

__ ECITAL

ART S __ OW

AM __ SEMENT PARK

BO __ FIRE

PAGEAN __

Answers on page 89.

FOLLOWING DIRECTIONS

Follow the directions below LINE BY LINE. Write the letters carefully on the blanks to change PHILADELPHIA to something else.

1. Write the word PHILADELPHIA

_____

2. Change the last letter to Z

_____

3. Remove all the vowels _____

4. Replace the first L with a J

_____

5. Insert three M's before J

_____

6. Remove the first two letters

_____

7. Place CF in front of the first M and in front of the last lette

_____

8. Remove the seventh, eighth, ninth, and tenth letters

_____

9. Insert SU in front of the last letter

_____

10. Put a space between the fourth and fifth letters

_____

11. Change each letter to the one that comes immediately before it in the alphabet _____

12. Switch the two words _____

Answers on page 95.

END/START

Put the answer to each clue in the column with the same number. Some words end in the center row across and other words start there. When all the words are in the grid, read across the center row to find the nickname for Alaska.

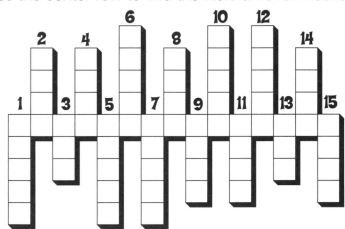

CLUES

1. The fattest finger
2. Tuna _____ sandwich
3. New Year's _____ (Dec. 31)
4. Show and _____
5. "_____ in Wonderland"
6. Board game with kings and queens
7. Salt water _____ (chewy candy)
8. Fifty percent
9. Make a sound like a lion
10. Another way of saying "Hi"
11. Organ of smell
12. Perspire
13. Frozen water
14. "_____ upon a time"
15. This is worn when you get out of the bath

Answers on page 86.

BEFORE OR AFTER

Change each letter to the one that comes immediately **BEFORE** or **AFTER** it in the alphabet to find a riddle and answer. Use this guide below.

ABCDEFGHIJKLMNOPQRSTUVWXYZ

VIBS   CP   ZNT   DBKK   UXN

_____

QHFR   XGP   MHWD   UPHDSIFS?

_____

OFO   QBMT.

_____

Now, do the same thing again to find another riddle and answer.

I P V   E N   S V Q S K D R   S B K J

_____

U N   F B B I   P S G F S ?

_____

C X   V R H M H   T G F K K   Q I P M D R .

_____

Answers on page 89.

SCHOOL SUPPLIES

Go through this maze and pick up each school supply before arriving at your locker.

Answers on page 92.

PUT ME IN

Add the word ME to each word in the box to make a new word that fits one of the clues. The word ME can be placed anywhere in the word—beginning, middle, or end. Do not change the order of the letters. The first word has been done for you.

CENT	COT	GAS	HARD
~~ROAR~~	SO	TAR	THE
	WARD		WON

1. Person who wanders   ROAMER
2. Heavenly body with a tail   _____
3. Ladies   _____
4. Concrete used for roads   _____
5. A few   _____
6. Topic of a story   _____
7. Reheated   _____
8. Person who works with lions   _____
9. Checkers and chess are board____   _____
10. Injured   _____

Answers on page 88.

COMPUTER CONFUSION

Circle the nine things that are wrong here.

Answers on page 91.

THE NAME GAME

Place one name from the box into the blank spaces on each line to form a word that fits the clue.

```
ANN    ARI    BEA    EVA
       LIZ    MAX
MIA    NED    RON    SUE
```

1. Ray of light   S U N _ _ _ M

2. Babysitter   N _ _ _ Y

3. City in Florida   _ _ _ M I

4. Soft paper   T I S _ _ _

5. Got some knowledge   L E A R _ _ _

6. The most   _ _ _ I M U M

7. Big snowstorm   B _ _ _ Z A R D

8. Help for the needy   C H _ _ _ T Y

9. Incorrect   W _ _ _ G

10. Lifting device in a building   E L _ _ _ T O R

TIME FOR BED!

Answers on page 92.

OUTER SPACE

Find and circle the seventeen outer space terms in the list. Look up, down, and diagonally, both forward and backward. Then take the leftover letters in the grid and read them from left to right and top to bottom to answer this riddle: **Why did the astronauts go to the doctor?**
For an extra challenge, you'll need to figure out where the spaces are between the words in the answer.

EARTH	NEPTUNE
ECLIPSE	NOVA
GALAXY	PLANET
MARS	QUASAR
MERCURY	SATURN
METEOR	STAR
MILKY WAY	URANUS
MOON	VENUS
NEBULA	

```
M F M Y X A L A G N
O E A R V T V H R E
H T R A E O E U M B
E R S C N N T E I U
I M A R U A B C L L
O E O T S R O L K A
S T P O S T Y I Y E
R E T E N A L P W S
N O H O Q U A S A R
U R A N U S T E Y S
```

Answer: _____

Answers on page 95.

PICTURE REBUS

Riddle: **What do you get if you cross a wolf and a rooster?**
To find the answer, name each picture and write it on the line. If there's a **PLUS** or **MINUS** sign after the picture, add or subtract those letters from the first word to make another word. Then read those words from left to right and top to bottom for the answer.

– M   – C +  – DE + – BL

_____   _____

T + – RP + - OE   – OK + – EL

_____   _____

W +   – CA + - SEP

_____   _____

– AW + – CP + - ET

_____

– NG + – GG + S

_____

Answers on page 91.

BIRD CATCHER

Two letters are missing from each word below. Write them on the blanks to answer the clues. Then read down the lines, two letters at a time, to answer this riddle: **Why did the sparrow fly into the library?**

1. Completely   __ __ T A L L Y

2. Storage area in a gym   __ __ C K E R

3. A U.S. state   __ __ L A H O M A

4. Flower with a trumpet shape   D A F __ __ D I L

5. Haircutter   B A __ __ E R

6. Swimming place   P __ __ L

7. Opposite of forward   B A C __ __ A R D

8. Head of a city   M A Y __ __

9. Cleans the floors   V A C U U __ __

Answer. _____

Answers on page 87.

WHAT'S COOKING?

Each of the foods below can fit in only one spot on the grid. Count the number of letters in each food to find the correct spot, ignoring any spaces between words. When the grid is full, read down one of the columns to find the name of another food.

FRENCH ONION SOUP

EGG ROLL

PIZZA

STUFFED CABBAGE

STEW

HOT DOG

FISH STICKS

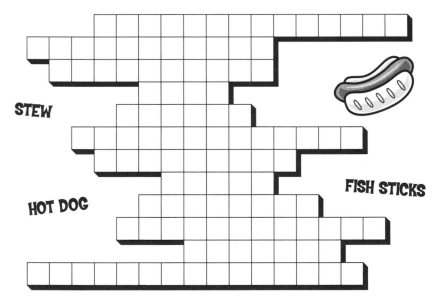

PORK AND BEANS

MACARONI

BACON BURGER

CHILI CON CARNE

SPAGHETTI

Answers on page 89.

LEFTOVERS

Almost all the letters of the words in Column A were rearranged to make the new word in Column B, but one letter in each word was left out. Draw a line from the word in Column A to the new scrambled word in Column B. Then write the unused letter in the space in the last column (next to the shorter word). When you're done, read down the column to find one definition for leftovers. The first one has been done for you.

Column A	Column B	Extra Letter
CHEAPER	DANGER	O
DEAREST	WORRIES	___
INFANTS	CLOSET	___
ANTLERS	NATURE	___
GROANED	REGRET	___
EIGHTHS	ALERTS	___
SAUNTER	SEVERE	___
DROWSIER	PREACH	___
GREATER	FAINTS	___
COLDEST	EASTER	___
DESERVE	HEIGHT	___

TRIPLE TREAT

Separate the list of vehicles into three categories: air travel, water travel, and land travel. Then put the words into the correct grids. Each will contain vehicles from one category only. A few letters were already placed to get you started.

AIRSHIP	CAMPER	PLANE
AMBULANCE	CANOE	RACE CAR
ARK	HELICOPTER	TRUCK
BALLOON	HOT ROD	TUGBOAT
BARGE	JEEP	VAN
BLIMP	JET	YACHT
BOAT	KAYAK	

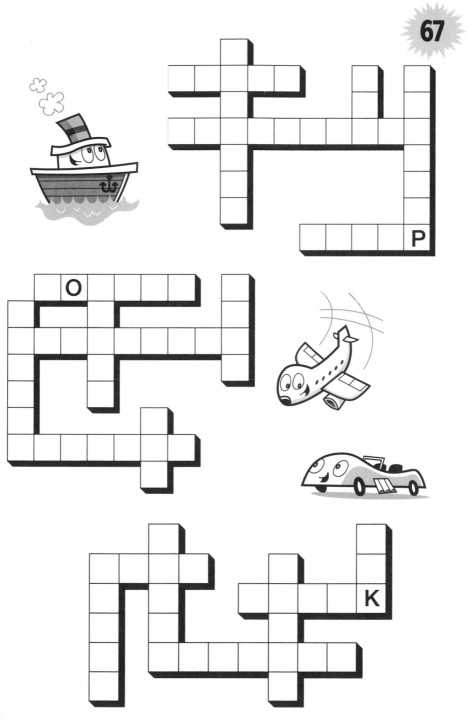

Answers on page 95.

SQUISH/SQUASH

Two related items are squished together on each line. All the letters in each word are in the correct order; you just have to separate them. The hints on this page list the categories of squished words, but they're in random order!

Example: LANGUAGES
D E N G U T L I C H S H =
DUTCH & ENGLISH

HINTS

Computer parts

Sweeteners

Fruits

Hot dog toppings

School subjects

Musical instruments

Olympic medals

Seafood

American states

Puzzles

1. C R J I O S S W G S O R D A W

_____ & _____

2. P B L A N U A M N A

_____ & _____

3. S I B R L O N V E Z R E

_____ & _____

4. M O D K E E Y B M O A R D

_____ & _____

5. R E M U L S T A I S R H D

_____ & _____

6. F I D G U I D T A L R E

_____ & _____

7. S H O U G N E A R Y

_____ & _____

8. K W Y A N O M S A I N S G

_____ & _____

9. S C I H I S E T O N R C E Y

_____ & _____

10. S C L H R A I M P M S

_____ & _____

Answers on page 86.

BLANKETY BLANK

Fill in the two blanks on each line to make a seven-letter word. Then copy the numbered letters to the same-numbered blanks in the answer line at the bottom of the page. Read across to find an expression that means "make a fresh start."

A R T I C __ __
$\quad\quad\quad$ 13 14

J O U __ __ E Y
$\quad\quad$ 3 4

N E P H __ __ S
$\quad\quad\quad$ 11 12

L I B __ __ T Y
$\quad\quad$ 7 8

G I R __ __ F E
$\quad\quad$ 15 16

N __ __ E L T Y
$\quad$ 5 6

G R __ __ O L A
$\quad$ 9 10

P I C __ __ R E
$\quad\quad$ 1 2

— — — —   — — — —   —
1 2 3 4   5 6 7 8   9

— — —   — — — —
10 11 12 13 14 15 16

Answers on page 96.

END OF THE LINE

Answer each clue with a five-letter word and write it on the blanks. Then read down the last column to answer this riddle: **What happens when cornstalks catch colds?** As a hint, letters have been placed on some of the blanks.

Bought with money   _ P _ _ _

Between fifth and seventh   _ _ _ _ _

Opposite of stay   _ _ _ V _

Mommy's husband   _ _ _ _ _

Fibbing   L _ _ _ _

Opposite of war   _ _ _ _ _

Ssh!   Q _ _ _ _

A sphere with a map on it   G _ _ _ _

"Pie" with dough, tomatoes, and cheese   _ _ _ _ _

Shaving tool   _ _ Z _ _

Bamboo-eating mammal   _ _ _ _ A

Type of power used by wizards   _ _ G _ _

Bismarck, _____ Dakota   N _ _ _ _

Not true   _ _ _ _ _

Material for windows   _ _ _ _ S

Answers on page 95.

SIXES AND SEVENS

Put together two word pieces from the box below to make a six-letter or a seven-letter word that answers one of the clues. Write each word vertically in the grid on the facing page. Be sure to match up the clue numbers with the column numbers on the grid. When the grid is full, read the circled letters in the columns from left to right to find the three-word answer to this riddle: **What did the sneezing champion get at the Olympics?**

ALO	ALS	BLE	BUFF	BUG
CIL	ETS	FAB	GAL	JACK
LADY	LETS	LOP	MUM	PED
PEN	PRI	RIC	VATE	WAL

CLUES

1. Small folding cases
for money _____

2. Material _____

AAAA-CHOO

3. Wild animal related to an ox _____

4. Run fast, like a horse _____

5. Colorful beetle _____

6. Speak softly and unclearly _____

7. Short coats _____

8. Bicycle parts _____

9. Not public _____

10. Writing tool _____

1	2	3	4	5	6	7	8	9	10

Answer: _____

Answers on page 89.

SOUND ALIKES

For each sentence, fill in the blanks with two words that sound the same but are spelled differently. Be sure to **WRITE** the **RIGHT** words. The first one has been done for you. The number of blanks tells you how many letters are in each word.

1. The P R I N C E and princess ordered extra
   P R I N T S from the photographer.
2. While the baker used __ __ __ __ __ to make a cake, the florist next door put a __ __ __ __ __ __ in a vase.
3. She never uses her __ __ __ __ phone, so she plans to __ __ __ __ it.
4. The gardener planted __ __ __ __ bushes in neat __ __ __ __ .
5. Look on the map to __ __ __ a river and a __ __ __ .
6. __ __ __ folks let us watch TV for one __ __ __ __ a day.
7. The kids __ __ __ their dessert at __ __ __ __ __ o'clock.
8. __ __ what if I can't use a needle and thread to __ __ __ on a button?
9. __ __ the way, we're going to __ __ __ new toys at the store.
10. The toddler did __ __ __ know how to tie a __ __ __ __ .

Answers on page 87.

MEMORY QUIZ

Study the picture on this page for one minute, then turn to the next page to answer some questions about it.

MEMORY QUIZ PART 2

Answer these questions without looking back:

1. How many people are wearing hats?

_____

2. What is the woman in the back doing?

_____

3. What is the woman in the front doing?

_____

4. How many people are using cell phones?

_____

5. What's in the cage?

_____

6. What does the baby have in its mouth?

_____

7. What's the freckled-face boy eating?

_____

8. What is written on the sign?

_____

Answers on page 92.

RECYCLING

People who work together to save the planet need to be able to give and take. Here's a puzzle that shows you how to do this. TAKE one letter from the word in Column A to make a new word without changing the order of the letters. Then GIVE that same letter to the word in Column B to make a new word without changing the order of those letters. In the last column, write the letter you gave and took. Finally, read DOWN to find out what some recycled plastic becomes. We did one for you.

COLUMN A	NEW WORD	COLUMN B	NEW WORD	LETTER
PEACH	_____	RICE	_____	_____
AMAZE	_____	PINT	_____	_____
TRIED	TIED	BEAK	BREAK	R
BOOK	_____	SUNK	_____	_____
BRISK	_____	TALE	_____	_____
NOTE	_____	VERY	_____	_____
NEATER	_____	HIT	_____	_____
CRUDE	_____	SOLD	_____	_____
TENTH	_____	SAVE	_____	_____
QUITE	_____	CRAM	_____	_____
WAIST	_____	MASH	_____	_____

Answers on page 94.

READ IT!

How quickly can you place each "readable" item in the grid? Start with the given letters and work from there until the grid is complete.

3 Letters
~~MAP~~

4 Letters
BOOK
CARD
MYTH
PLAY
POEM
SIGN
TALE
TEXT
YARN

5 Letters
ATLAS
DIARY
ESSAY
FLIER
PAPER
STORY

6 Letters
COMEDY
LETTER
RECIPE
SPEECH

7 Letters
MYSTERY
OUTLINE
PROFILE

8 Letters
BROCHURE

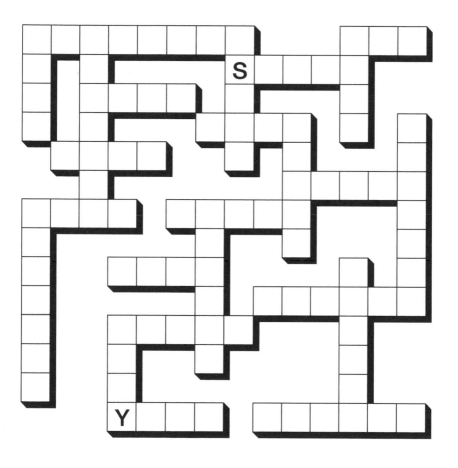

Answers on page 94.

SOME DIFFERENCE 2

Circle ten differences between the picture on this page and the one on the opposite page.

Answers on page 91.

FOUR FITS

Place one of the four-letter words from the box below into the blanks on each line to make words that fit the clues. Each of the words will be used only once.

EATS	LOSS	ONCE	PEAK	RAVE
ROLL	SOUR	TIRE	URGE	VERY

1. E _ _ _ _ W H E R E   In all places

2. M I S _ _ _ _ I   A Midwestern state

3. S T _ _ _ _ E D   Walked slowly

4. C _ _ _ _ R T   Musical show

5. F _ _ _ _ E S   Uses dental string

6. S _ _ _ _ O N   Doctor who operates

7. S _ _ _ _ I N G   Talking

8. S W _ _ _ _ H I R T   Soft, long-sleeved pullover

9. T _ _ _ _ L I N G   Taking a trip

10. E N _ _ _ _ L Y   Completely

Answers on page 95.

TREE OF KNOWLEDGE

Put the nine scattered words into the grid horizontally and in alphabetical order. Then read the circled letters from left to right and top to bottom to answer this riddle:

What's the smartest tree in the forest?

BROILER

BALANCE

BELLHOP

BARBERS

BLINKER

LOSSOM

BEDTIME

BUNCHES

BOTTLED

Answers on page 94.

GOOD ADVICE

Answer each clue in Column A with a five-letter word. Answer each clue in Column B with a four-letter word. On each line, there will be one letter in the first word that is NOT used in the second word. Write only this letter in the third column. Then read down to find the three-word answer to this riddle: **What's the best way to talk to a monster?**

COLUMN A

COLUMN B

EXTRA LETTER

1. Round dishes for soup

Not fast

— — — — —

— — — —

— — — —

2. Shouts

Opposite of buy

— — — — —

— — — —

— — — —

3. Very mean

Make healthy

— — — — —

— — — —

— — — —

4. Misplaces

— — — — —

5. Not fancy

— — — — —

6. Parts of books

— — — — —

7. Used a laundry machine

— — — — —

8. Veggie that makes you cry

— — — — —

9. Glide on ice

— — — — —

10. Boy or Girl Scout unit

— — — — —

11. Furniture with a flat
top and legs

— — — — —

12. Work of fiction

— — — — —

13. Center parts of apples

— — — — —

14. Type of syrup for pancakes

— — — — —

Fewer

— — — —   ——

Bucket

— — — —   ——

Small green veggies

— — — —   ——

Go on a horse

— — — —   ——

Twelve o'clock

— — — —   ——

Grab

— — — —   ——

Opposite of rich

— — — —   ——

Item worn on
the waist

— — — —   ——

Cherish

— — — —   ——

Flower with thorns

— — — —   ——

Tropical tree

— — — —   ——

Answers on page 90.

ANSWERS

DIRECTIONAL SIGNALS
(p. 33)
Answer: CAN I GIVE YOU A LIFT?

MEETING POINTS (p. 50)
1. TWENTY
2. COUCH
3. MOUSE
4. BEARD
5. NINE
6. TRAY

Answer: BECAUSE YOU CAN'T IRON THEM.

SQUISH/SQUASH (p. 69)
1. CROSSWORD & JIGSAW
2. PLUM & BANANA
3. SILVER & BRONZE
4. MODEM & KEYBOARD
5. RELISH & MUSTARD
6. FIDDLE & GUITAR
7. SUGAR & HONEY
8. KANSAS & WYOMING
9. SCIENCE & HISTORY
10. SHRIMP & CLAMS

FOUL BALL (p.16–17)
1. REPORTER
2. PLATTER
3. POCKETBOOK
4. JIGSAW
5. DIFFICULT
6. BOULEVARD
7. SUPPER
8. COBRA
9. MAYBE
10. PICCOLO
11. PORTRAIT
12. RELAX
13. SEPARATE
14. SHALLOW
15. CABIN
16. UNHAPPY
17. TERRIBLE
18. COURAGEOUS
19. QUIET

Leftover words: SHY MAN SWAY FROG SHE WALL.
Riddle answer: SHE RAN AWAY FROM THE BALL.

END/START (p.53)

Answer: THE LAST FRONTIER

IT'S NOT WHAT YOU SAY . . .
(p.34–35)
1. Big deal
2. Hang in there
3. Banana split
4. Short story
5. Sweep it under the rug
6. Quarterback
7. Double park
8. Left-handed
9. Jack in the box
10. Just between you and me

BIRD CATCHER (p.63)
1. <u>TO</u>TALLY
2. <u>LO</u>CKER
3. <u>OK</u>LAHOMA
4. DAFF<u>O</u>DIL
5. BAR<u>B</u>ER
6. P<u>OO</u>L
7. BAC<u>KW</u>ARD
8. MAY<u>OR</u>
9. V<u>A</u>CUU<u>MS</u>

Answer: TO LOOK FOR BOOKWORMS.

LETTER BOXES (p.5)

Answer: A WALKIE TALKIE

ICE IS NICE (p.7)
1. CIRCLE	8. PIECE
2. DICE	9. POLICE
3. JUICE	10. PRICE
4. KITCHEN	11. PRINCE
5. MICE	12. RICHER
6. NICKEL	13. WITCHES
7. OFFICE	14. SWITCHES

STARTERS (p.12–13)
LOS	INK
FEBRUARY	ALLIGATOR
EASEL	THUNDER
ITALIAN	DENTIST
AUGUST	SATURDAY
FREE	DESSERT

Answer: FIT AS A FIDDLE

SOUND ALIKES (p.74)
1. PRINCE/PRINTS
2. FLOUR/FLOWER
3. CELL/SELL
4. ROSE/ROWS
5. SEE/SEA
6. OUR/HOUR
7. ATE/EIGHT
8. SO/SEW
9. BY/BUY
10. NOT/KNOT

READING ROOM (p.36–37)

1. SOUTH	7. BROWN
2. HANDS	8. CRY
3. YEAR	9. BITE
4. FOOT	10. BAKE
5. AIR	11. LOUD
6. BEAR	

Answer: WHERE DO YOU FIND BOOKS ABOUT TREES? AT A LIBRARY BRANCH.

PUT ME IN (p.57)

1. ROAMER
2. COMET
3. WOMEN
4. CEMENT
5. SOME
6. THEME
7. WARMED
8. TAMER
9. GAMES
10. HARMED

TWOSOMES (p.26–27)

Answer: CHOPSTICKS

DOUBLE TROUBLE (p.29)

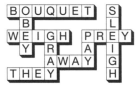

SOUND OFF (p.18)

Answer: NOISEMAKERS

CLOSE CALLS (p.28)

MISTAKEN
HAIRBRUSH
CALENDAR
FAREWELL
TRIPLETS
TREASURE
BREAKFAST
Answer: BEST FRIENDS

TIME OFF (p.51)

F E S̲ T I V A L
C O N C̲ E R T
P A R A̲ D E
C A R N I V̲ A L
L E̲ C T U R E
C O U N̲ T Y F A I R
M A G̲ I C S H O W
R O D E̲ O
R̲ E C I T A L

A R T S H̲ O W
A M U̲ S E M E N T
P A R K
B O N̲ F I R E
P A G E A N T̲

SIXES AND SEVENS
(p.72–73)

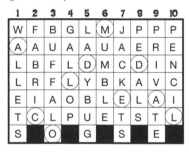

Answer: A COLD MEDAL.

STEP BY STEP (p.23)
HOW DOES A CHICKEN MAIL
A LETTER? IN A HENVELOPE.

WHAT'S COOKING? (p.64)

Answer: FRIED CHICKEN

BEFORE OR AFTER (p.54–55)
WHAT DO YOU CALL TWO
PIGS WHO LIVE TOGETHER?
PEN PALS.

HOW DO TURTLES TALK TO
EACH OTHER?
BY USING SHELL PHONES.

GO FIGURE (p.45)
24 = H
13 = L
2 = T
15 = S
30 = N
20 = C
7 = W
4 = A
10 = E
3 = Y

Answer: THE SCALY NEWS.

QUICK CHANGES (p.31)

FLAME/FRAME	R
PEDAL/MEDAL	M
SWEAT/SWEET	E
MARKS/MASKS	S
FALLS/FAILS	I
HIRED/TIRED	T
MONTH/MOUTH	U
BRAND/BRAID	I
SMALL/SMELL	E
RAVES/SAVES	S
RIGHT/NIGHT	N
GUEST/QUEST	Q
CURVE/CARVE	A

Answer: IN TIMES SQUARE.

WAKE-UP CALL (p.20)

NECT<u>A</u>RINE	BICY<u>C</u>LIST
ATTE<u>N</u>TION	MISP<u>L</u>ACED
	GRAD<u>U</u>ALLY
COMP<u>A</u>NION	DEMO<u>C</u>RACY
KNOWL<u>E</u>DGE	CHEE<u>K</u>BONE
SIGN<u>A</u>TURE	
GEOG<u>R</u>APHY	
CHIP<u>M</u>UNKS	

Answer: AN ALARM CLUCK.

FRONT OF THE LINE (p.19)

<u>H</u>ILLS	<u>H</u>IDES
<u>E</u>IGHT	<u>O</u>PENS
<u>A</u>DDED	<u>N</u>INTH
<u>D</u>REAM	<u>C</u>HALK
	<u>H</u>EELS
	<u>O</u>CEAN

GOOD ADVICE (p.84–85)

1. BOWLS/SLOW	B
2. YELLS/SELL	Y
3. CRUEL/CURE	L
4. LOSES/LESS	O
5. PLAIN/PAIL	N
6. PAGES/PEAS	G
7. DRIED/RIDE	D
8. ONION/NOON	I
9. SKATE/TAKE	S
10. TROOP/POOR	T
11. TABLE/BELT	A
12. NOVEL/LOVE	N
13. CORES/ROSE	C
14. MAPLE/PALM	E

CLOCKWORK (p. 40)

CLEAREST	C	RELATES
ARTICLES	I	SCARLET
CRACKERS	K	SCARCER
CREATURE	U	TERRACE
EPISODES	O	DESPISE
SHUTTLES	T	SLEUTHS
MATTRESS	T	STREAMS
OPERATED	O	TAPERED
PLATTERS	T	PLASTER
READINGS	D	ERASING
REGIMENT	M	INTEGER
CRUMBLES	C	SLUMBER
RELEASED	E	LEADERS
SMOOTHER	O	THERMOS
THICKEST	H	TICKETS

Answer: IT TOCKED TOO MUCH

SOME DIFFERENCE 2 (p.80–81)

COMPUTER CONFUSION (p.58)

PICTURE REBUS (p.62)
Answer: AN ANIMAL THAT HOWLS WHEN THE SUN RISES.

ADD-A-LETTER (p.8)

T
AT
ATE
HATE
HEART
HEATER
CHEATER
TEACHERS

PICTURE CROSSWORD
(p.24–25)

FAMILY ROOM FUN (p.44)

THE NAME GAME (p.59)

1. SUNBEAM
2. NANNY
3. MIAMI
4. TISSUE
5. LEARNED
6. MAXIMUM
7. BLIZZARD
8. CHARITY
9. WRONG
10. ELEVATOR

SOME DIFFERENCE (p.46–47)

MEMORY QUIZ PART 2 (p.76)

1. None
2. Talking on a cell phone
3. Holding a baby
4. One
5. A bird
6. A pacifier
7. A hamburger
8. No littering

SCHOOL SUPPLIES (p.56)

SECRET CITIES (p.41)

1. SANTA CL<u>AUS TIN</u>KERED IN HIS WORKSHOP. (Capital of Texas)
2. WILL THEY SHIP THE GAZE<u>BOS TONI</u>GHT? (Home of the Red Sox)
3. IS THE GAR<u>DEN VER</u>Y BEAUTIFUL? (Capital of Colorado)
4. SHE'S FR<u>OM A HA</u>RBOR TOWN. (Largest city in Nebraska)
5. BUY A <u>STAMP A</u>T THE POST OFFICE. (City on the west coast of Florida)
6. THEY MADE A C<u>HART FOR D</u>AD. (Capital of Connecticut)
7. <u>JUNE AU</u>CTIONED OFF HER BOOKS. (Capital of Alaska)
8. CAN THE AUTH<u>OR LAND O</u>NE PLANE? (Florida city with many tourist attractions)
9. GIVE THE ADMI<u>RAL EIGH</u>T DOLLARS. (Capital of North Carolina)
10. THE SCAN<u>DAL LAS</u>TED A LONG TIME. (Texas city whose nickname is "Big D")

FILM CLIP (p.38 – 39)

SAFETY FIRST (p.15)
WHAT DO GHOSTS DO WHEN THEY GET INTO A CAR?
THEY FASTEN THEIR SHEET BELTS.

94

READ IT! (p.79)

TENNIS ANYONE? (p.21)

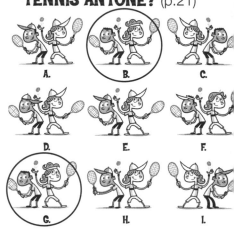

FIVERS (p.43)

Musical instruments	Body parts
1. BUGLE	1. BRAIN
2. FLUTE	2. ANKLE
3. CELLO	3. HEART
4. PIANO	4. MOUTH
5. BANJO	5. ELBOW

RECYCLING (p.77)

EACH/PRICE	P
MAZE/PAINT	A
TIED/BREAK	R
BOO/SKUNK	K
RISK/TABLE	B
NOT/EVERY	E
EATER/HINT	N
RUDE/SCOLD	C
TENT/SHAVE	H
QUIT/CREAM	E
WAIT/SMASH	S

TREE OF KNOWLEDGE (p.83)

B	A	L	A	N	C	E
B	A	R	B	E	R	S
B	E	D	T	I	M	E
B	E	L	L	H	O	P
B	L	I	N	K	E	R
B	L	O	S	S	O	M
B	O	T	T	L	E	D
B	R	O	I	L	E	R
B	U	N	C	H	E	S

Answer: ALBERT PINESTEIN

CLOTHES ENCOUNTERS (p.9)

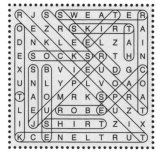

TRIPLE TREAT (p.67)

OUTER SPACE (p.61)

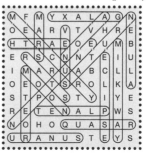

Answer: FOR THEIR
BOOSTER SHOTS.

END OF THE LINE (p.71)

SPEN<u>T</u>   GLOB<u>E</u>
SIXT<u>H</u>   PIZZ<u>A</u>
LEAV<u>E</u>   RAZO<u>R</u>
DADD<u>Y</u>   PAND<u>A</u>
         MAGI<u>C</u>
LYIN<u>G</u>   NORT<u>H</u>
PEAC<u>E</u>   FALS<u>E</u>
QUIE<u>T</u>   GLAS<u>S</u>

Answer: THEY GET EARACHES.

PICTURE RIDDLE (p.42)

A. VEST   D. WITCH
B. HANGER   E. BABY
C. DESK   F. PIRATE
Answer: A VERY BIG
DISHWASHER.

FOLLOWING DIRECTIONS (p.52)

1. PHILADELPHIA
2. PHILADELPHIZ
3. PHLDLPHZ
4. PHJDLPHZ
5. PHMMMJDLPHZ
6. MMMJDLPHZ
7. CFMMMJDLPHCFZ
8. CFMMMJCFZ
9. CFMMMJCFSUZ
10. CFMM MJCFSUZ
11. BELL LIBERTY
12. LIBERTY BELL

FOUR FITS (p.82)

1. E<u>VERY</u>WHERE
2. MIS<u>SOUR</u>I
3. S<u>TROLL</u>ED
4. C<u>ONCER</u>T
5. F<u>LOSSE</u>S
6. S<u>URGEO</u>N
7. S<u>PEAKI</u>NG
8. SW<u>EATSHI</u>RT
9. T<u>RAVEL</u>ING
10. EN<u>TIREL</u>Y

HOUSE HUNTING (p.6)

ON THE OUTSKIRTS (p.22)

1. LOUDEST
2. SEVERAL
3. WEAKEST
4. BARBELL
5. FIXABLE
6. CONTEST
7. DECIDED
8. RUBBISH
9. REQUEST
10. THICKEN

RIGHT ON "Q" (p.49)

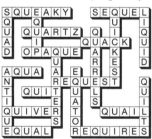

BLANKETY BLANK (p.70)

ARTICLE
NEPHEWS
GIRAFFE
GRANOLA
JOURNEY
LIBERTY
NOVELTY
PICTURE

Answer: TURN OVER A NEW LEAF.

OUT OF SIGHT (p.10-11)

LEFTOVERS (p.65)

GROANED/DANGER   O
DROWSIER/WORRIES   D
COLDEST/CLOSET   D
SAUNTER/NATURE   S

GREATER/REGRET   A
ANTLERS/ALERTS   N
DESERVE/SEVERE   D

CHEAPER/PREACH   E
INFANTS/FAINTS   N
DEAREST/EASTER   D
EIGHTHS/HEIGHT   S